. . . I've heard your feelings

Also by Theta Burke

SOUNDS OF YOURSELF

AND WE HAVE TOUCHED

*SANDCASTLES AND CUCUMBER
    SHIPS LAST FOREVER*

*LOVING WHO YOU ARE WHERE
    YOU ARE*

WHEN YOU CAN'T SEE A WAY

*CONNECTIONS
    (PERPETUAL DESK CALENDAR)*

WHISPERS TO MY SOUL

... i've

heard your feelings

theta burke

Delafield Press   Suttons Bay, Michigan 49682

Library of Congress Catalog Card Number: 76-7103
Copyright © 1976 by Theta Burke
All rights reserved
Printed in the United States of America
First Edition
ISBN: 0-916872-00-9

For all those I love
who have shared with me parts of themselves
and who continually contribute
to my becoming
And for all those who will take the time
to look within.

I've heard your feelings . . .

about becoming

about love

of some pain

about loving

just about life

1.

about becoming

one.

I open to you
only those doors to me
which I can trust your entering
with acceptance

But at times that trust
        may be so tenuous
as to allow only the unlatching
and there needs be a gentle push
as you knock.

two.

I am Me
but they do not see.
I am to them
          what fits their perception
and they look not beyond
to my reality.

three.

The desperate intense searching
      for what is real
      for what is truth
      for what is me
One points here
another there
and I look until the exhaustion engulfs me
and makes me feel there is no truth
      no me
I am tortured by the thought that within
is what I fear to see
And there seems at times
to be a thousand me's.

four.

What is within
and what is without
are so intertwined
as to sometimes appear indistinguishable
and one's actions are too often determined
by conflicts between the two.

To gain knowledge and understanding
of the parts of the self
allows energy spent in conflict
to be used
       in growing
       and in giving.

five.

No doubts
        (inadequate awareness)

Doubts and questions
        (growing)

Doubts and questions with faith
        (wisdom)

six.

How else is judgment learned
but by risking?
Some right decisions are made
and some wrong ones
but these can only be viewed in retrospect
(and actually should not be judged as right or wrong).
One's footing needs practice
        so that the steps become more sure
When the goal is to climb the mountain
a slip or fall shall not deter
The journey need not be hurried

There is time.

seven.

Sometimes the reaching
for *something*
feels safer and more predictable
than allowing oneself
to risk the reaching
for *someone*

But the risking
        is the key
to the far greater treasure.

eight.

Interdependence I think
is better than independence
Total dependence is not — cannot be — now
Was it ever felt
Or was the lack of it long ago
what causes the fear of some of it now?
The protection and security that some dependence "feels"
is not forbidden
but is necessary
      for the inside growing
while the outside is meeting necessary responsibilities
and going toward a chosen goal.

The security of some dependence is the cushioning
for the hurting and doubting times
      which are a part of growth
and for some resting along the way
Learning to use the cushioning
      and feeling comfortable with it
is not regression
but a route to progress
      and mature interdependence.

nine.

When I was a child
I didn't like asparagus
      or split pea soup.
It was beyond my comprehension
that ever I would
but now I do.

ten.

Words and emotions
trigger flashbacks
        of earlier feelings
and cause current reactions
to be a response
        not to what is meant
but to earlier perceptions
than make *then*
        seem *now*
when it is not.

Will you continue to cling
        to the dream of what *was*
so that the substance of what is now
is shut out?

eleven.

For a long time I felt like a Cinderella
with my reality among the cinders
while I fantasied about the glass slipper.
Nothing was accomplished
until I learned I could be
        my own fairy godmother
And all things became possible.

twelve.

Searching
and learning the freedom to sort
to choose what parts of me I want to keep
and those parts I reject.
To be
      and become what is me
to find what pleases me
How shall I choose?

The road is new
       and I feel uncertain.
I will learn the way
       but how?
I must find a way to unload the guilt.
Perhaps learning the freedom to choose *is* the way
For what is the guilt but feeling unable to be
       a way chosen or expected by another?

In my becoming you will be at times
        a dumping ground
        a mirror
        a giver or a receiver
to help me see and become me
as I allow
        while I choose.
But I need to know that you are there.

thirteen.

Emotions learning expression
are like unto a young bird
being pushed from the nest
     vulnerable in infancy
but growing in strength
as the elements are met
and contended with
gaining security that experience provides
learning the freedom to soar
     into the open sky
or to rest
     on a pine bough.

fourteen.

I saw you being the way you are
heard you saying ways you felt
and I learned to be me

fifteen.

From the deepest recesses of my being
comes the yearning
and I ache with longing
for all that was not.
A part of me feels as yet unborn
         an embryo
and the rest as thirsty as a desert.
Dare I allow some help in the birthing?
Is there anywhere the gentle strength
for the complete acceptance
of whatever the newness might produce?
Can anyone know the fragility and vulnerability
of what might emerge?

Perhaps because with you I sense love
in a way I have not known
I can have hope of its being
          as I want to know it.
I will let me be born
and you are the mother of that part
Need those others hurts be named?
They were of the longing for existence
and as I know within me the nurturing needed
for the newborn — and on
I will become what is me
and learn a secure freedom.

sixteen.

Traveling back over long forgotten roads
trying to make the pieces of the mind's puzzle fit
rousing sleeping memories
     and unfulfilled yearnings
to make some sense and purpose
to *now*

seventeen.

How does one stretch
        the certainty of a moment
into enduring confidence
if the hours and days
        of the heart
are not allowed
        their just accumulation
of past achievements
and the knowledge of love
from those yesterdays?

eighteen.

Look within
What needs be seen is
     what has been
       what is
         and what can be
As these are learned
the charting of your course may be altered
But you shall be the navigator.

nineteen.

I knew what I was
before I became
Time and experience it took
to cause more of the outside to appear
as the inside long before was felt.

There can be no rushing
of this accomplishment
And those who too quickly
judge what is us
miss much.

I shall continue to become.

2.

about love

one.

As the marsh fog
is lifted and absorbed
       by the morning sun
so is aloneness
dissipated by the warmth
       of love.

two.

How fortunate are those who are aware
of the riches of relationships
Among such there can be no real poverty.

three.

Would that those I love
never feel an obligation to do
      or to be
other than what is an expression
of themselves.
The greatest tribute I can know
is for another to feel the comfort of himself
with me
and to know that what I might feel toward him
is not diminished should his pitcher hold less than mine
      at a given moment
each of us giving freely of what we are
and neither demanding more.

four.

Reach out
for only by your reaching
does the other know
he matters to you.

five.

Did you ever notice a dry sponge
        all stiff, inflexible and unusable?
As it absorbs water
it becomes able to fulfill its function.

Love does that to people.

six.

When great love is stored in the soul
there is heightened perception
to the smallest bit of it in others
and faith in its potential for growth.

seven.

What power is real?

To direct the actions of men and empires
seems insignificant
as compared to helping influence *one*
learn to love.

eight.

Love listens
and attends to whispers
      of thoughts and feelings
which the self may not
      have yet acknowledged.

3.

of some pain

one.

The restlessness within
makes no place a haven.

When shall I know peace?

Where does one find a resting place
from himself?

two.

The rejection I imagine from you
is but a reflection
of the unhappiness and uncertainty
I feel within.

three.

Hurt I knew before I could name the word
hurt that I somehow felt responsible for
and guilt for having caused.
My penance is to suffer
and not rebel.

When will I know there is no crime
for which I have to pay
and feel my chains unloosed?

four.

Sometimes I say I hate you
because I'm afraid
      you don't love me.

five.

Detached I feel
apart from people
an onlooker.

I want to feel in the mainstream
a part of
not apart from.

To cross the chasm is the goal.

To feel a part of the whole
allows the freedom to be apart from
and still a part of.

six.

There were the three of us
my parents and me.
In my long ago infancy
I could not discern
that I had less power to affect their moods
than they mine.
And when they were sometimes angry or sad
I felt responsible.

So I learned guilt.

seven.

In my early growing
all love and all pain
seemed as one
with no Divider to help me perceive
      or distinguish
so that an appropriate response
could be learned and expressed.

And I shut out *all* feeling
because the anguish of uncertainty
was too great.

eight.

How can you stretch
and know the comfort of yourself
when yourself has not been expressed
to you or to others
without the shroud of guilt
inhibiting?

nine.

Until you can see me with all my guilt
(that perhaps you see no reason for)
Until you can let *that* me be
(suffering as I may feel the need)
I will be unable to risk allowing myself
freedom from the guilt.

ten.

Is not the pain of growth within
enough?
Must there be those who stand over
and point to our suffering
Condemning?

That is but the way of those
not attuned to the inner turmoil
who have not the sensitivity
        and patience
to let our being emerge.

eleven.

Sometimes a hurt is so sensitive
that naught can come near
save the softness
        of understanding silence.

4.

about loving

one.

Tonight I feel loved
and I say to myself
I hope those *I* love know and feel it.
That's very important, you know,
that your love is believed—
else it's like an outstretched hand
with no one there to grasp it.

two.

How shall my heart be certain
of that which you feel for me
when you are away?

The reassurance of your nearness I need
until I learn that love knows not the bounds or limits
      of distance.

three.

You may not be what I want tomorrow
but today I can be all of me with you
and that's something new.
I would like to be to you
what you need, too,
while it lasts.
And I hope neither of us will be too hurt
when we no longer need each other.

four.

From one I love
I ask much
because I care much.
That which I ask
is not more than you are
but what you are.

five.

In sweeping waves
let not your love come to me
overpowering
but gently
while I learn
lest I lose my tenuous footing
and be lost in the sea.

six.

My knowledge of the love you have for me
cannot exceed the awareness of love that I have known
from those who loved me before you.

As I learn your love
it shall be added to that which I feel
and will be able to give
to you
or to another.

seven.

My restless wandering spirit
is like a butterfly
unable to find a lighting place
when things with you
are uncertain.

Absences I can handle
if things are right
and there's no misunderstood communication.

eight.

When my heart is lonely
the warmth of your body
says all to me I need to hear
And the silence of my love
speaks more than could all my words.

nine.

You are never so close
as sometimes
      when you are away.

ten.

You stood apart
and said I should not come near
My heart
        listening to yours
heard a different message
But I was afraid
and listened to the words.

eleven.

The hardest thing in life?
To love and not be loved I once thought.
But does not love felt and given
eventually realize its purpose?
For in the loving, do we not give that
which will cause one loved
to better know
        even if at some later time
a fuller realization of another's love?

Now that I have learned this truth
the pain I feel is more bearable
and I find comfort in the hope
that I have added some bit
to your future deeper joy.

twelve.

I am as a sea whose current
is an extension unto you
and its reception
is a confirmation
        of myself
as it invades the stillness
        of you
to cause a merging.

thirteen.

'Tis sad to feel a love die
to feel the warmth and tenderness fade
and be replaced
by a lost directionless emptiness—
an unwanted freedom.

Where does one go between loves?

Does the tree know in winter
it will bud again in spring?

fourteen.

Because I love you
my awareness sees beyond
      that which you speak.

fifteen.

If everybody loved everybody
would that not be sad?
For then I could not choose to love you
or you to love me.

sixteen.

You
someone to dream with
and share
        shadows and sunlight
        laughter and tears
        anguish and relief
and serenity.

5.

just about life

one.

The heart and the mind
in joint concert
express the harmony of life
as the hands of the pianist
blend and interpret a melodic composition.

two.

At one with things as they are
knowing that they as we
are in the eternal process
of becoming
And only as we are attuned
to the overall purpose
does any portion of being
make sense.

three.

The degree of our joy
in the accomplishments of others
is in direct relationship
to our security and happiness
with our own efforts.

four.

Sometimes if things have to be said
something is lost in the translation.
There are times
       when silence speaks best.

five.

On yonder mountain shines the sun.
From the rising to the setting
its light falls in varied shadows
at different times of the day
But that does not mean that either the sun
        or the mountain changes
or that they who describe them differently
are liars.

six.

Work there needs be for a man
that does not furrow his brow
in burdensome distress
work that he gladly meets each day
spending himself freely
confident that his labor is not in vain
e'en though the harvest be distant.

seven.

Live not in fear
of ill health, disaster or doom.
Energy spent in such
detracts from the power of self-renewal
and contributes to that which is feared.

eight.

Those who truly help us
are they who provide an attitude
wherein we may become aware of
        and accept all that we are
so that we learn to realize the strength and power
of that self.

nine.

To the wounded who lie in pain
we do not speak of the joys of health.
To feel and accept their pain
is the best comfort.

ten.

He holds to himself possessions
who has not known
riches of the spirit.

eleven.

Real giving
is never just an exchange
or a response to a perceived obligation.
But because you gave
        I give
sometimes to you
        and sometimes to another.

Mostly the gifts I like
are thoughts.

twelve.

One must spend that which he is
so that he may become more.

thirteen.

I must ever be watchful
lest my life become encumbered
     with irrelevance
I must remain at the helm
     of my ship
My cargo must be that
which allows for cruising
in the waters I choose
unfettered by extraneous weight.

fourteen.

Often the voice of certainty
is more strident and audible
when the responsibility
lies elsewhere.

fifteen.

Ill will toward oneself
is usually a result
of avoiding knowledge of that self.
For knowledge brings understanding
and understanding begets acceptance
which eliminates hatred of self
or of others.

sixteen.

Times there are
when I must step aside
        from the throng
Some things along the way
        I need more time for.

I must not allow those crowds ahead
or those that push from behind
to determine my pace.

seventeen.

Good relationships make of life
a ship secure to sail any sea.
If perchance the timbers break
and are swept away by the waves
that which built the ship
shall continue to be.

eighteen.

When the tide is in
and life is full
our soul is expressed
          in the living and the relating
At ebbtide come the reflections
and expressions of
          the joys
              the loneliness
                  or despair
And we wait again for full tide.